T0157124

WHO IS THE
FIRST-CLASS GHANAIAN?

WHO IS THE
FIRST-CLASS GHANAIAN?

A Story of Tribalism, Religion, and Sectionalism

in Ghana and the Way Forward

ALBIN AKANSAKE

iUniverse, Inc.
Bloomington

Who Is the First-Class Ghanaian?
A Story of Tribalism, Religion, and Sectionalism in Ghana and the Way Forward

iUniverse books may be ordered through booksellers or by contacting:

iUniverse
1663 Liberty Drive
Bloomington, IN 47403
www.iuniverse.com
1-800-Authors (1-800-288-4677)

ISBN: 978-1-4759-8537-5 (sc)
ISBN: 978-1-4759-8538-2 (ebk)

Library of Congress Control Number: 2013907059

Printed in the United States of America

iUniverse rev. date: 04/16/2013

CONTENTS

PREFACE

My intention to produce this book came up first when I ran for the post of local National Union of Ghana Students (NUGS) secretary at the University for Development Studies (UDS), Tamale, Ghana, as well as during my subsequent contest for the position of general secretary at the national level. Numerous issues arose during the campaign, especially at the local level. Although the election is supposed to concern student activism, many people were voting based on which part of the country the contestants came from. I am therefore not surprised when I see some of these tribal loyalties reflected in our national politics. However, I still have faith and hope that this practice can be minimized, if not eliminated. For it to be reduced or stopped completely, everyone has got to play a role as a leader with respect to the people who are under his or her influence, through our daily conversations, our one-on-one talks, our public speeches when we are called to deliver them, our writings, and our deeds. I regard it to be part of a citizenship obligation to put these things together in writing here, especially relating it to my own life as someone who plays a pivotal role as a student activist and who belongs to the two major sections of the country and thus crosses the north and south dichotomies.

I hate politics of tribalism and discrimination, and that is exactly the status quo of Ghana. Politics of tactics and a Machiavellian kind of politics prevails whereby politicians believe that defaming their opponents and denigrating their reputations will provide them with opportunity to capture political power. Little do they realize that those comments have the tendency of sending our beloved nation into chaos. Respect, as they say, is reciprocal. This book will therefore help such people to value one another no matter which part of the country they come from, what food they eat, their particular economic background, or their religion, and it will endorse a transparent politics that is devoid of insults and personal attacks. For, at the end of the day, we have only one Republic of Ghana, a nation regarded as the beacon of African democracy, and the hope that, during a difficult time, we can represent the hope of Africa—as the black star in our national flag truly stands for.

Financial problems deferred the publication of this book, and things are still not well with me. Day in, day out, I battle within myself, especially the case during this year's campaign for national election and during the results when properties were destroyed and the opposition even had to go to court to challenge the transparency of the results: a problem I consider to be purely tribal. Although I left the country to further my studies in the United States, my interest has always been to know what is going on in my country. Because, out of site, is not out of mind, Many people live our country to countries like the United States where there are many opportunities and turned to forgot about their own country, but I always believe that collectively, we can also make our own country even more than this, though, as a poor student who couldn't provide food for myself during my school days and have to visit offices of government officials before I pay my school fees, life turn around for me in just less than two years in the United States, I bought my house in Accra, sponsored the production of this book myself, own three private cars, and expecting my baby in just some few months, just to mention a few. I did not let proud overtake me just because of who I am now, but still setting my mind back in my old days, and thinking about how to help that widow and her son full of potential but lacking money to pursue his dreams, and roaming in the street of Accra and have twisted his life for truck pushing, he is the reason why this book is published. I kept reading people's articles and opinions published on the Ghana web, I listen to online radio every morning, I watch online television, and I even make phone calls directly to find out what is going on just to keep myself updated. And as I keep following panel discussions by representatives of various political parties as well as their campaign speeches, I wonder why such people should even call themselves "politicians" because the comments are frequently disgusting and frustrating.

However, the issue is not me being annoyed. That I listen to them and feel revulsion does not solve the problem; it cannot change the mentality of the people. I therefore deem it necessary to address this book not only to the current politicians but also to my colleagues and to the rising stars who look up to them as mentors, asking them to have a different mindset and to understand the rules of the game, especially as is necessary in a multicultural country, such as ours. The book does not only educate but also serves to caution by citing examples in Africa and in some other parts of the world that suffered genocides as a result of occurrences similar to what is happening in our country today. Examples include the Rwandan and Darfur genocides, the apartheid in South Africa, and even the Holocaust that occurred in the 1930s.

As a proud northerner and later becoming adopted by my beloved new family of Akan descent, I spent much of my life with two different tribes. I have also spent time in the field as a result student, with rural people in the northern region when I was pursuing my bachelor's degree at the UDS. I would not say that my experiences have made me a genius in the area of politics, capable of offering advice to folks from the various tribes to forge unity. However, I believe my experience can take away some small percentage of doubt from folks who are ethnocentric in nature; we all pledge allegiance to one national anthem as Ghanaians, not as northerners or southerners. We should therefore embrace the things that unite us and keep us going as a nation. Politics has always suggested division, but it has been particularly bad in Ghana politics; the nation is divided in terms of religious groups, ethnicity, civil society, pressure groups, and sectional ties. A small nation of twenty-three million like ours consists of more than forty different tribes, with each and every tribe claiming superiority over the other, and a broad array of diverse religious groups, such as Christians, Muslims, Hindus, and Jews. The divisive nature of the country is a true reflection of our political process; that is to say that if you are not from the wealthier tribe you cannot be a president even if you qualify. And it is not just in politics but in sports also; the question of who should lead the national team remains tribal, hence our low performance in football in the late 1980s and in the 1990s.

This book is mainly based on my personal life story, at the centre of the two major sections, and my experiences of both cultures. It tries to address the challenges that exist between them. Little has been referenced from people's articles and opinions, or from newspapers and magazines, or the media documentaries shown on television, especially concerning the various types of genocides that have been cited.

As it talks about my life, it also unveils my belated single mum, Faustina, aka sister Fausti, whose sudden demise occurred in August 2005. Fausti's life on earth was marked by tragedy. She lost her husband when I was one. As a single mum, her aspirations for her children to have a better education were too high; she wouldn't care to trade her cloths for our school fees. She did not have any formal education, but she could read and write, and, by profession, she was a petty trader and a peasant farmer. She never had a high-paying job in her life, but she never saw me or my siblings sleeping with hunger. Many of the stories narrated in this book were told by her. I remember that she used to say that she did not care if her children graduated from school and she dies and that happened. Indeed, my brother graduated on 28 July 2005, and she died on 28 August that year—exactly one month after his graduation. I strongly believe that this book would have contained more than this had she lived to see this day. She always made me understand that society can never do without conflicts and that fighting conflicts of interest in order to protect self-reputation is part of the norms of society. I therefore have no doubt about the status quo.

I don't want to describe the deep nature in which I still mourn the personal loss. Regardless, I still see her as the most generous woman and one with the most spectacular spirit any woman could ever wish to have. My siblings and I still owe her a lot, and I believe that giving and helping the poor, which were her values, is the only way to pay her back in spirit.

My father, Patrick Azipala, who has become more of a myth to me than a father, also had a great influence over my experience through the stories told to me about his sudden demise by my mum.

My partner Abena, who is an Akan from the other section of the country, has extended my knowledge about the cultural variations, especially when there is a quarrel between us.

I also want to say a special thanks to my granddad, Mr Alexis Anongu, and to his wife for their financial support in my schooldays, as well as extending a special thanks to my siblings, Vitus, Olivia, Yayaa, Akosua, Akua and my unborn baby.

Gratitude goes out to Mary Apeka, my aunt, to Thomas Akampieh, and to all the readers of this book.

The main reason why every anti-tribal preacher and visionary person would wish to have a copy of this book is that the book does not only outline the tribal difference and its likelihood of leading the nation into chaos, but it also reminds us of what has happened in the past and its consequences in some parts of the world.

The divisive nature of our country also accounts for the country's economic upheavals; for instance, the attention of every sitting government in Ghana has always shifted to what it has called its "world bank", thus the region or the constituency that voted massively to bring it to power, thus meaning the unequal and unfair distribution of the national cake.

The book also discusses great empires and kingdoms that fell or suffered from genocides as a result of divisions based on race, religion, and ethnicity. The goal was not to write a history book—or rewrite history—but I deemed it necessary to remind ourselves and the country about what happened elsewhere and its possible consequences. Out of those genocides, lives were lost, poverty became the order of the day, young people could not achieve their dreams, and women and children became more vulnerable in society.

In the same vein I know that folks are familiar with most of the stories I tell in these pages. I am not trying to be professorial in this book, but to err is human, so others may have forgotten and may need to be reminded.

I have witnessed how desperate and anxious people are when a nation goes into such a situation, for instance, the loss of lives in Kenya, Liberia, Sierra Leone, and Rwanda, and the murder of more than six million Jews—mainly children—during the Holocaust. That is not to forget the women who were assaulted in Ghana. Men cut women's breasts while they were still alive, and there were all kinds of assault during a tribal war Between a section of the Moslem groups in Wenchi, a community in Ghana.

Even if I hadn't seen events with my eyes, I read about how conflicts in Liberia in 1996 twisted the lives of children there and manipulated their destinies, many seeking refuge in Ghana. I still have friends who were victims. I think it is the responsibility of every citizen in our nation to avoid similar occurrences. For this purpose this book was published.

INTRODUCTION

Following almost a decade of hiding my identity as a 100 per cent northerner, or "pepeni" as the Ashanti will call it, I finally came back to my senses when I arrived in the United States, got a job and had to work with a Whiteman. He is the best racist I have ever encountered. As soon as I got hired at Worldpac, I was posted to work with him, but, even as coworkers, wherever I stood, he would not stand close to me. Neither would he touch me. If I touched some of the work equipment and he happened to touch it also, he would wash his hands, numerous times. He didn't do this to me alone but to every black guy who worked with him.

That was not the only encounter with racism. I visited my friend on the weekend at Montclair in New Jersey. Thomas was a graduate student at the university, and we went to the campus football court to participate in the ongoing games during the weekend. When we entered the field, we found that the whole place was overcrowded, so everyone had to sit very close to one another. We sat near three white girls and then pushed closer to them in order to fit ourselves. They pushed away from us. As we kept pushing, they finally got out and left the place; they just did not want to sit close to us.

When I got home, I reflected on the two experiences, and I felt less human. It made me remember a time long ago when I refused my own people. After I was adopted, I saw my own people as inferior just because I had been brainwashed thus by my new family. Having all of these experiences, from the local to the international, I believed it would be a good idea to write a book about tribalism in Ghana since my experience was a perfect example, and I believed it would be good material for those people who still lack the wisdom of age, as I did those years back.

In those moments, ignorance engulfed me, and I thought that it was an attempt and a desire to protect my identity from scrutiny. Little did I know that I was insulting nature, as I was naturally born a northerner.

That also battled within myself was the idea of exposing myself and my life to the public domain, particularly my past, which in some ways I consider to be shameful. This is not because I have a "bad record" or that I regard my ethnicity to be bad, but because this book speaks mostly about my personal life story and my family, which sometimes reminds me of my sorrow. I mean especially the tragic demise of my beloved parents, which occurred at an early age, and the struggles in my life thereafter.

The book is all about memoir, histories, and family experiences, and links are drawn in the text between particular aspects of my life. I have also paraphrased some parts of articles that were published on the web, especially the Ghana web. The reader should find any direct quotations to be accurately cited and referenced. I obtained some information from documentaries that were showcased in the media, particularly on the BBC, on CNN, and on the "History".

Some characters that appear in the book represent a change from reality in the purposes of protecting privacy. Similarly, some of the spellings of names that appear in the book represent intentional misspellings.

MIRIGU

At the age of six, my mother wanted me to start going to school. She enrolled me into a local school. However, back then I used to hate waking up early in the morning. Sometimes my parents would have to resort to singing songs to try to coax me from my bed. Little did I know that going to school was a privilege and that it was very essential to my future. My mum would sometimes tell me that if I showered and went to school then upon my return she would buy me food and new clothes. I soon realized that these promises were all simply tricks and ruses.

I recall one particular week day when I woke up and my mother tried to convince me to go to school. "Albin, do you see that jersey of Abedi Pele that Thomas wore when you guys were playing soccer yesterday?" she asked.

"Yes," I replied.

"I will buy you a nicer one if you go to school today," she said.

"No I am not," I responded. "Unless I see it, I won't go."

From that day onward she stopped trying to get me to go to school by offering nice rewards and resolved instead to beat me until I got up and got ready for school.

My brother Vitus and I walked to school every morning. As I would already be filled with frustration on this walk I would take it on any children who would play around with me to beat them.

* * *

The norm in Ghana schools is for every school to have a parade for announcements before marching to classrooms with marching songs. In Nabango L/A Junior High School, the parade song went like this:

> Good morning, good morning, good morning, Mr Awini
> Good morning, how are you?
> I come to make a complaint
> About the Ashanti people
> The people of Ashanti
> They have no sense
> When the gun is fired
> They cry bue, bue
> Bue, bue, bue, bue, ajieeeebue
> Buebue, they cry buebue.

I never understood the meaning of this song until one day when I arrived home from school and asked my grandmother Azina about the lyrics. When I sang the song she laughed and asked why I was so interested in it. I kept insisting that she told me about its origins and meaning though, and eventually she started to talk me about the old days when the colonial masters arrived in Ghana.

My grandmother said that the colonial masters first settled along the Cape Coast, all the way to Kumasi (historically spelled as "Comassie") in the Ashanti region. She informed me that their main aim was to spread the gospel of Jesus Christ to the infidels (evangelism). Later, their attention shifted to trading; they adopted a system of trade called "the barter system of trade" where goods were exchanged for goods. Because at that point the black man had not yet discovered what is known today as "money", they would bring finished products, such as cooking utensils, items of clothing, and silver pans for fetching water from the bole holes to be exchanged in return for rich mineral resources, that is, gold, diamond, bauxite, and iron.

In those days, black men used to cover themselves with fresh leaves from trees and with locally manufactured cloths called "malleats".

"Malleats" were made by taking out the body of a fresh tree and beating it as fresh as it was until it became softer and then mixing it with some chemicals. These later graduated to become what is called "kente", which is a local wear in Ghana until date.

The white man later discovered that black men were of sufficient strength and capability to be brought to the West for farming in the "Green revolution". White men therefore started to buy slaves, later using force to bring slaves that were resistive. That was the period when they started showing guns and other ammunitions that the Ashanti man had not seen before. When the "warning shot" was fired just to intimidate the black man, they could be known to scream, in loud voices and in the local dialect, "Bue, bue, bue" and "Ajeei, ajeei, ajeei," which means, "Ahh, Ahh, Lord, Lord, Lord". When the other tribes later came to discover this story, they used it to mock the Ashanti tribe, claiming that they responded as cowards.

This was an even later story, but the original gun mockery started with the Fantes. And even today, the Ashantis themselves use it as a mockery tool against the Fantes. When the white man originally arrived on the African soil, their first contact was at Cape Coast, at the southernmost tip of Ghana, an area occupied by the Fantes. The Fanti people used to cry at the sight of the guns because they had never seen them before. Colonial masters used to gather the Fanti people together in a room in which there was also a gun. As the people were afraid they would remain in the room the whole day. The colonist used to tell them that if they left the room the gun would turn on them and shoot them. When they wanted to use the urinal, they would bow to the gun and say, "Magyaotu, mpakyew me pe de me koagya nan ba anti oyaa mentum," which roughly translates to, "My Lord gun, I want to use the restroom; please don't shoot me."

Over time the colonists discovered gold and cocoa in Ghana. In the Ashanti land they extended their territory. When they shot their guns in the Ashanti land the people would run around shouting, "Agyae, agyae, agyae!" meaning "Oh my goodness!" The song about the Ashantis came into being because of their coward behaviour. The song is more of a tribal song to denigrate the Ashanti tribe.

3

*   *   *

As a child I didn't know that there were any tribes apart from the Fafra tribe, so the story that my grandmother told me did not concern me that much. I was more concerned about my rice after school. In the northern region, not all families were able to feed their children three times a day. Some families had to eat rice only yearly during holidays like Christmas and Easter. As the climate changes, the desert keeps invading the northern part of Ghana and, coupled with their single raining season, farmers harvest crops only once a year. Most of the farming is peasantry, so food scarcity and chronic poverty are major issues in the northern part of Ghana.

As I got older I began to gradually gain wisdom and to differentiate between many things. When I visited my friends and I saw their families, I would always see my friends' fathers living with them, that is, with the whole family, as a household. So one day I decided to ask my mother about my father. When we were sitting down one day I asked, "Mum, who is my father?"

She was surprised at the question, and she bowed her head down for a while. Finally, she replied, but with a question of her own. "Albin, what made you ask this question?"

"Well, I have been going to my friends' houses, and I always see them with their fathers and families, but when I come home I have no one to call 'father'. So where is he?"

"Your father has travelled to Yeji [a city in the Brong-Ahafo region of Ghana], where he was born," she informed.

"So when is he coming back?" I asked.

"I don't know, sweetie."

Every morning I would start to cry because I wanted to go and see my father. My mother's friend Azoya came to her one day and told her to tell me the truth. So on the next morning my mother called me outside to sit with her on a traditional stool. Then she began:

"Your father was born in Sirigu, a village in the Upper East Region of Ghana, to a 42-year-old woman. The woman had already gone through the menopause, and she had difficulty conceiving children. Her husband lived in Yeji [a settlement in Kenya's Coast Province] and was a security guard. The couple tried diligently to have children, but when it did not happen then they went for help. They went to a herbalist and a traditional healer in Mirigu [in the Upper East Region, too, and not far from Sirigu] who happens to be your granddad. The herbalist told her that he could only help her if she got married to him. She agreed and married him, and together they had a son called Azipala. Azipala was your father, and his name meant 'no one knows your destiny'.

"He grew up in Yendi [in the northeastern quadrant] and attended school there, but he returned to Mirigu to practice as a people teacher. He wanted to save some money for college. That was around the time that I met him.

"We started dating and got married. In 1982 we had our first baby boy, and that was your elder brother, Vitus. We had you later, in 1986. As for many new couples, it was difficult for us to depend on your father's salary. Your father used to go to Yedi at times to work as a 'by day' or 'paa'. In the year after you were born there was a day when he embarked on his usual routine journey, but he never returned back. I heard he died of heart disease and TB."

My father, whose life had been a complete mystery to me, now became real. This was especially so when my mother said that I was a complete photocopy of him. My physical features and my behaviour were apparently a replica of his, and that is why they had called me Albin, a name deriving from the word "Albinism".

My mother had another child, Olivia, with her boyfriend. As a mother of three children life became tougher for her, and she considered moving south to make a better life for herself and her family. However, since the north had a paternal system, the family did not want her to move with her children. In the middle of one night, she ran away with us.

She put me in a silver pan and carried it on her head. She carried my sister on her back. My older brother walked to Natugnia [in the Upper East Region].

ASONKWA

We finally settled in Nkoranza, a district of Brong-Ahafo, where my mother's father lived. The main source of income for her father's family was farming. Living in Brong-Ahafo was life-changing, as it was the beginning of my tribal experience.

In my village I went to school with people of a different background. I met people from the Frafra tribe and people from the Akan tribe. I found out that the Akan people had difficulty understanding me when I spoke. They would make fun of me and even call me "ante boi", meaning someone who did not understand their language.

Whenever they called me "ante boi", I responded by calling them "kambombi-zorigo". This phrase meant that Ashanti boys had no common sense. Because of the parade song at Nabango L/A Junior High School I believed at this point that Ashantis were cowards and that they had no common sense.

As I continued at the school, eventually I started to speak in a way that was understood, and I began to adopt parts of the new culture. I dropped some of the northern mentality and picked up some of the southern mentality. However, instead of things getting better as I grew and matured, it got worse. I started to know the meaning of terms like "ta ni", "pepeni", "sremni", and "aboa", and the rest, which were all Akan tribal bigotries used to make fun of the northern tribes.

These terms were annoying, and I found myself agitated whenever I heard them, because I had the mentality that Ashantis were not human beings. In the north I had heard stories about the Ashantis being dwarfs with tails. I had heard that by nature they were very short, but when they started having affairs with northerners they procreated normal human beings. So my mind was full of these lies and false stories. It is like in the north they paint a black picture of the Ashantis and, in the south, they paint a black picture of the northeners.

BIREM

Such tribal comments did not end at this point, as I then moved to Birem in the Ashanti region to attend my primary six there. In Birem I came to realize that ethnocentrism does not only exist for the Akans and for the northerners, but that also between the Akans themselves are in existence the beliefs of certain groups in their superiority. The Akan itself is a large tribe made up of the Ashanti people, the Fantes, the Akuapem, the Bono people, the Ahafo people, the Nzema people, the Akyem, and many more. Although these Akan tribes have similar cultures and almost a similar language, there are still numerous differences that exist between them. Tribal comments levelled against one another are not only between the Akans and the northern tribes but between the Akans themselves, with each tribe claiming superiority over the others. When it comes to electing a national leader, each tribe would also like to have a representation, which is practically impossible, and is something that always causes great political tensions, although Ghana is considered to be the beacon of Africa's democracy.

BADU

The four years I spent in the Brong-Ahafo region enabled me to understand the language commonly used there. So when I got to Badu, I met Ashantis who mocked me when I spoke their language. Throughout my one-year stay in Birem I was known as "maatwa" instead of "matwa". This originated when our teacher, Mr Addae, marked our class assignment and distributed it to the class, and I had one question marked wrong. My friend Nkrumah had provided the same answer, but his was marked correct. So after comparing it to his I tried telling Nkrumah that mine was marked wrong, saying, "Weimaatwansowaati me." Meaning, I had it right, and the teacher marked me wrong.

I also remember from this time a single song that almost generated a tribal war between the Ashantis and the Brongs. It was a song called "Yefri Tuobodom ye capital town ne Gyenegyene"; it gave an avenue for the Ashantis to make fun of the Brongs in Kumasi. When people came from Techiman and the nearby villages to transact businesses in Kumasi the Bono people felt insulted, and, out of anger, they would retaliate with insults.

Because things were not going in my mum's favour as she tried her hand at petty trading, she made the decision to go back to Nkoranza to her father. However, I was left behind with Mr Francis, a Roman catechist, because I was a good mass servant and a Bible reader. In fact, I was the only child among the group of children who could read the Twi version of the Bible. And, as is typical of rural communities in developing countries, adult illiteracy was high, so whenever the reverend father came around they had to look for me to read the Bible in both morning devotion service and in the daily mass service, at the age of 11. However, I later joined my mother because I couldn't be away from her for too long.

I started JSS, but as all of my friends and classmates were migrating to towns like Techiman in the hopes of getting a quality education, I also started to desire studying in the city. It was believed that those who studied in the cities achieved higher scores to gain entrance into better schools than those in the villages. I told my mum of my wishes, but she told me that she could not afford to pay for fees in the city. The only option my mum saw as being left was to send me to my granddad, who lived in Badu and who was the district circuit supervisor of education.

Badu is a community in the midst of Brong-Ahafo, but it has its own native language—Kolango, or badu language—that is different from the language that is spoken in the rest of the Brong-Ahafo region.

I started JSS and, as usual, tribal comments rose up. Tribalism in Ghana is practised in almost every household. Even as children, we were faced with tribalism, for example, in the election of a class prefect. I understood this when our class teacher, Mr Effah, dethroned our class prefect by the name of Christian and asked for applications from members of the class for a new prefect. No on applied but myself, and thus Mr Effah came to class one day and instated me automatically as the new class prefect. I was faced with challenges and insults from my co-students. They questioned why a "dagaree" or a "frafra" should lead the class. Instead of focusing on my abilities they judged me on the basis of my tribe. The question I always wanted to ask myself is which tribe is it that has been endorsed by our constitution to inherit leadership. I resigned my position as class prefect because of the lack of cooperation.

WENCHI

Two years later I had passed my Basic Education Certificate Examination (BECE), and I was preparing to go to high school. My mother could not pay for boarding fees, but she provided instead for me to rent a room at Wenchi, a private hostel with low charges in comparison to boarding fees. Living in Wenchi was a wonderful experience because it exposed me to so many things in life. I had a wonderful intercultural experience. I had thought that ethnocentrism and the use of racial comments only existed among the children, the illiterates, and the villagers. However, little did I know that even educated elites are also ethnocentric.

A man by the name of Mr Dadzi, an elective maths teacher, was teaching class one afternoon. As he was explaining mathematical problems, he stated that solving a maths problem is like looking for a "ta ni" and happens to come across "Aso". He said that you should not bother asking where the "ta ni" is upon meeting the "Aso" but should just continue on your journey, and you would surely meet the "ta ni" on your way. He basically meant that "Ntafo" are mostly farmers in the villages; they are always identified by their hoes and cutlasses. Therefore, if you are looking for a northerner, you will meet the hoe and then eventually you will meet the northerner.

It represented a denigration of the northern community of the class, and it caused confusion between northern and Ashanti students as they tried to look down on each other. The teacher of the class, someone who was supposed provide an example for his students, was rather entertaining such ideas. When will tribalism and racism not be a threat to our security, as for what our founders fought? Three brave men laid down their lives because of the injustice and maltreatment by the colonial government. They did not die for one tribe; they died for Ghana and its social justice. So why is our nation divided in our days?

*   *   *

My first academic year of high school ended successfully, and I went back to the village. When I arrived home I found that things had changed since the last time I had been there. My mother was sick and very weak. She did not have the means to go to the hospital, so she had resorted to taking local herbal medicine and praying for a return to good health. However, she got worse. One day she was rushed to the hospital. She died there of malaria and asthma.

The next morning my brother Vitus and I were talking about girls when my grandfather came to the house and called my older brother outside. "Vitus, Vitus, Vitus," he said.

"Ba baa," Vitus replied.

"Your mother just died in Techiman Hospital."

We both got up and started crying, to be joined in our tears by a crowd of people who understood what we were going to have to face. Elder people knew what our mother's death would mean for us. As a young person I felt it, but not as much. I began going through hell shortly after her death. I was faced with the challenges of feeding myself in the school and buying clothes for myself.

The funeral nights were performed as tradition and custom demanded, and I returned to school. I had just lost my mum, and I had no dad, but my mind was still full of big hopes and dreams of a better future.

I didn't have the food that I had been used to, not to talk of paying for Parent—Teacher Association (PTA) dues and other fees. My rent was also outstanding. The following week my landlady came and asked me to pack up my things; she needed the room. I asked if she would do me a favour. She asked what it was. I bowed down my eyes in shame and told her that I had lost my mum during the holidays, and, I did not have a father because he had died when I was very young. She said that she understood but that the house was not an orphanage home, and thus she couldn't do anything about my predicament.

When the landlady had gone I closed the door to my room, and I laid down on my bed. My mind quickly turned to memories my mum. Thoughts of committing suicide began to blow over my mind. As still young, I thought the only remedy to my plight would be to resort to drinking. I started drinking.

There was a moment when all hope had finished; I thought that I was left only with the choice of becoming a street boy, a drop out, a thief. However, I quickly told myself that I was going to persevere, whatever the case. I told myself that even if I had to sleep outside I would still attend the school because I could see myself living up to my dreams spiritually. However, how it would materialize was questionable.

As the Bible said, the stone that the builders rejected has become the cornerstone. In reality it was my life rather than just a biblical story. The same Ashantis that I had learnt during my childhood to be dwarfs, to lack common sense, and so on, had adopted me in my time of need. As a good child—even before I knew what was to befall me in the future—I had been helpful to the elderly people in my jurisdiction. When I saw MaameAkosua Manu coming from the market I would always collect her belongings, escort her to her house, pound her fufu-an Akan traditional food, and help her with household errands.

In my mind, I was providing a hand to another human; little did I know that I was working for my own good in the future. When I was thrown out by my landlady, I became stranded in the city of Wenchi, and Maame Akosua adopted me. It was not just to stay in her home and to go to the school but to be part of the family. Soon outsiders could not differentiate me from Maame Akosua's family. People thought that I was the biological son of Maame Akosua and, until today, when people ask me I sometimes say that I come from Wenchi. As long as I am Ghanaian I hail from every region and city of Ghana.

Despite all of the good treatment given to me as "pepeni" in Maame Akosua's house, there is no doubt that tribalism and the use of provocative words to widen racial differences were issues during my stay at Maame Akosua's house.

My stay in Maame Akosua's house provided me with some insights into how some Akans perceived northerners and other tribes in Ghana. Any child who did not like bathing or who was always dirty was insulted as "wo ho fiise tani", meaning "your dirty body like a northerner". Any violent person in Akan society was referred to as a northerner (although the person was an Akan). When there was any irrational behaviour on the part of an Akan man in Akan society it was questioned whether the person was of northern descent—because, to them, an Ashanti person is not supposed to behave irrationally. The northern tribes were denigrated to the extent that I began disassociating myself from my fellow northerners due to the lack of knowledge and my nurturing experiences. As boys, when we would go out to meet ladies I would tell the women that I was from Ashanti in order to try to win the affections of the Ashanti ladies.

*   *   *

The sudden change of mentality and the anti-northern behaviour I encountered had a negative consequence on me. When I went to the university in the Upper West Region, I had left Wenchi again, and I had gone back to the north for my university education. And the whole story began changing, but this time around it was shifting towards the middle. That was the time that I actually began to discover answers to my long-awaited question: Who is the first-class Ghanaian? As an adopted Ashanti, I moved into school at the UDS, and all of my friends were Ashanti. I stopped speaking my own language, even when I met with my own people. One time I made up my mind to run for an executive position as local NUGS student leader. There I realized that the issues of tribalism, religion, and sectionalism were not just issues in our national politics but even in student activism.

All of the northerners denied me votes just because I had associated myself with the Ashantis and had identified myself to be a southerner.

My only support came from the Ashanti students, who represented the minority. Hence I suffered my first electoral defeat with only 87 votes. Feasibility studies showed that my defeat was also in part a result of my religion. I was a Christian, and my contender was a Muslim, hence his advantage.

This issue of tribalism not only played a central role in the NUGS election but in the Student Representative Council (SRC) as well, whereby a northerner won the election because of how he spelled his name. In Ghana, various tribes are identified by their last names, and my friend's name, if one letter were to be replaced, would become an Ashanti name. He won the election against his fellow northerner with southern popularity because he changed his name by replacing it with one letter, and people could not identify his exact tribe, so he had votes across all tribes.

There was a time when even renting a room in Wa was determined by racial background. If you were from the north then you would get a northern discount, but if you were a southern student then you would have to rent a room for a higher amount.

One morning I went to a public Kumasi Ventilated-Improved Pit (KVIP) (sanitation facility) in Wa, and I found that I had no coins with me. The KVIP attendant would not allow me to use the facility until he discovered that I was a northerner, and then he passed me through. Upon my return, I questioned why it was that he would not have allowed me to enter when he thought that I could have been an Akan. He said that it was because when he went to Kumasi they did not respect him and thought of him as an animal. "Why should I favour them when they fall into my trap?"

I was personally not satisfied with the explanation, although I was myself a northerner, because I wanted him to have said that they were favouring the northerners because of the poverty. Comparing the different tribes on campus then I had realized that the southern students (and not only the Ashantis) lived in good conditions compared to my counterparts. Giving myself as an example, on my first day at Wa as a fresher, I found that I had only GH¢ 20 (Ghana cedi), and I had not paid any rent. I had only paid my fees and the costs to transport myself to school. I got to Wa at about 2 p.m., and I got stranded. I went with a friend to his house, but he gave me conditions as to when I had to leave his room. The next morning, I didn't have the money to take the "trotro", and I walked about 5 miles before I located a catholic church. After church I started approaching people and laying down my problem before them. Those who were not moved by my story walked over me. However, one widow, who could picture the futures of her own children in the event of her absence, took me to her house and accommodated me for one full semester before I was able to raise sufficient money to rent for myself a room.

As the saying goes, "Cut your coat to suit your cloth." I never cut my coat to suit my cloth while I was at the UDS. I didn't always have food to eat, but I still told myself that I was going to run for local NUGS office, and I made it happen. I was determined, and people saw the enthusiasm and helped to finance the whole campaign until its end. And I did run the most expensive campaign, and I even ran at the national level for general secretary of NUGS after the local election. However, I did not live to see the results of the national election, as my visa to the United States was expiring. I resigned from my candidacy.

My decision to run for the national office of NUGS happened because I always believed in hope and determination. That is, I believe that in this life if you are not a pessimist, and if you are determined to work hard, no dream will be too heavy and will prove too hard to achieve. No matter your colour, your race, the food you eat, the language that you speak, how your last name is spelled, the values that you hold, or your culture you are entitled to the basic universal opportunity of possibilities.

I also debunk a popular adage in Ashanti language that "yewowo to sie so a, wonkye ten tene ye", meaning that if one is born on top of a mountain, he or she easily becomes tall. I do not believe that destiny is determined by family income status. Gone are the days when we could push the blame for our situations on to our fathers. Your family may not have had the money to send you to school but through the popular success formula awaits success, preparedness, and opportunities.

As the semester was drawing to an end, and since that semester was the last semester of the academic year, all denominations were preparing to hand over leadership positions to the incoming seniors. Our church also had its executive election on that same weekend service. Even in the church, racism and tribalism play central roles.

*   *   *

On campus we had so many religious denominations, namely, for example, PENSA, CATSU, PAX ROMANA, GHANSU, APOSA, and CASA. As a choir member of the Charismatic Revival, I woke up, brushed my teeth, took a bath, polished my shoes, and got dressed. All set, I called, "Yeboah? Yeboah?" and waited for my roommate to respond before telling him that I was going to church.

The popular means of transportation to the church was a motorbike. If you did not have a motorbike then you were not regarded in the same light as those that did. The motorbike riders would pick up their girlfriends and leave us behind. If they saw you standing by the roadside, waiting for a lift, in the main they would simply drive by and blow dust over you. Sometimes you would get a good Samaritan who would stop and offer you a ride. Here I came, without "trotro" money, dressed up and standing by the roadside, looking for a lift. They passed me by.

I was still standing in the sun looking for a motorbike lift when my roommate called me on my phone. He said, "Are you still standing on the road? I am in the white car that just drove off."

"Oh, OK," I replied. He said that I was a miser, presumably referring to the fact that I was waiting for a motorbike, as it was the only way that I would not have to pay.

The truth of the matter was that I was not being an economizer or whatever they call it; I simply didn't have the money. He knew that, but he was just making fun and creating jokes. He understood what I was going through because he lived with me.

Finally a lift came. My friend Kamara, who is also a church member, had been late setting off that day, and his girlfriend had not waited for him, so he had space on his bike. When I saw him I shouted "Kamara! Kamara!" He responded to urge me on to his bike, I jumped on, and away we went. By noon, mass was already coming to an end, with people engaging in short euphoria: dancing, clapping, jumping, and singing.

> "We offer sacrifice of praise,
> Into the house of the lord.
> We offer sacrifice of praise,
> Into the house of the lord."

Once we were done with the short enjoyment, the priest offered benediction and said that we could now continue with the second part of the service. The outgoing secretary called on all of the aspirants to deliver a short message to include making clear why they believed that the audience should vote for them. To me, Bright, who was an Akan, delivered many pleasant surprises in his short speech and should have been voted into office. However, to surprise, the election went the other way around.

People questioned at the end of the service why one should come from the south to lead in the north. So I wondered if even in the church elections on tribal lines also existed.

As this campus election was almost at the end of the semester we were soon vacating the USD, and I was to come back to Wenchi.

*   *   *

As an adopted child from a different ethnic background, the elderly from the house understood the frustration I would feel if tribal bigotries were used against my northern tribes, so my colleagues in the house were always mindful of their tongues to spare me and to make my living there comfortable. I would not have lived there with them because of the disregard for my tribe if I had had a viable alternative, because no one wants to hear negative things about his origin. However, in all I knew I had a big dream to accomplish and that dream to me was beyond the insults and other comments.

TECHIMAN

One day, I paid a courtesy visit to my extended family who live in Techiman. On my arrival, I witnessed a sad situation. My cousin had decided that she was ready to make a life with an Ashanti man she had met. He was the manager of a popular hotel in Techiman, and he was a very handsome, wealthy, and humble man. They were preparing for a gargantuan wedding. However, her father had discovered that she was going out with an Ashanti guy, and he was cursing her. "You are not going to marry that guy or else you will never have my blessing in that marriage."

They finally had to separate and terminate the relationship based on racial and tribal grounds. This cousin of mine was almost 30 years old then. She told her father that if she was not to marry that man then she would never marry any other man on earth. Her father said that that outcome would be better than marrying an Ashanti man.

Until today, she is still not married. She cannot find someone who is one of her tribe mates who she loves. Meanwhile our Christian faith teaches us that what God have put together, let no man put asunder.

The next morning of my stay in Techiman, I got up early in the morning, as it was a Thursday, the special day set aside for the Wenchi market. I had to go back to my family in Wenchi to help them in the market preparation since the household income largely depended on business transactions during those market days.

When that day's market was over it was time for the boys to hunt women. The classmate of my best childhood friend Benjamin (Ben) Yeboah had come to him, and I fell in love with her.

However, the first day I met her and heard her conversations with Ben, everything suggested that she was tribalistic and that she would not like me since I was not a biological Ashanti but adopted. My assumption was based on the fact that, my adopted brother Kofi had put a cloth on his neck, and the girl I admired secretly asked him why he had tied the cloth like he was a "ta ni"—a term used to describe those from the north, and suggesting that anything awkward or abnormal should be from the north. In discussions with Ben, I planned to deny my northern tribe for the sake of love.

I took her number that day, and I called her. The next morning I was already beginning to propose to her. I said, "maame Julli, how are you?"

"I am great by his grace," she replied.

"Oh, I do nothing but think about you all night," I said.

"Really? I thank God that I am so very important to somebody to make him stay awake," she answered.

"Oh, don't say that, ohemaa." In the local dialect that means, "Pretty girl, you are very important."

"Don't begin telling this for your girlfriend to beat me." I knew from this that things were going to be positive.

"I don't have a girlfriend because I have never met any girl I love in this world except you." She laughed.

"By the way where are you from?"

"Oh, I am from Wenchi here. My grandmother is Maame Akosua, but my mum is dead. She died some years ago."

"Really?"

"Yes."

"Oh. I'm sorry for that."

You cannot cheat nature. You can run from God, but you cannot hide from God. Although I was claiming to be an Ashanti for the sake of the affection of a woman, my accent revealed that I am not a complete or biological Ashanti.

"But your accent doesn't suggest that you are a real Ashanti."

"Oh, I was raised in Badu, and my dad is from Badu, but my mum is from Wenchi." Badu, as I said earlier, is a small town near Wenchi. The people of Badu have their own language, which is different from Twi.

By playing with her intelligence and linking myself to the people of Badu, I won the girl. We hung out for a couple of months, and she got closer to me. One day she requested to know my full name, and I told her that my full name was Albin Amoah. I denied my own identity. My last name, Akansake, remained hidden, as, in Ghana, someone can determine another person's identity by knowing their last name.

One day I went out with her, and I met my classmate who called me Akansake, instead of my first name Albin. The guy shouted, "Hey, Akansake!" I didn't respond, and I pretended that I had not heard. "Hey, Akansake!" came a second time. I did not respond. My classmate drew nearer. "Hey, have you forgotten that your name is Akansake, or what? Is it because you are walking with a lady?"

I finally admitted the truth about my origins to the girl, and that was the end of our relationship. We broke up, as she did not want to date northerners. With time I came back to my senses that no matter where you come from, your culture and your values should never be hidden. All human beings—be them white, black, Akan, northerner, Ga, or Voltarian—are equal in the eyes of God.

*   *   *

After vacation, we were asked to attend our usual third-trimester practical program. While I was on the program, in Gambibgo, in the Upper East Region, I had a call from my grandfather. "Albin, did you enter a draw for this American lottery?"

"No," I responded because I could not remember exactly when I had entered a lottery.

"Ahh, maybe it's a scam."

Two days later the lottery agent called my granddad again. This time around my granddad was not far from convinced that it may be authentic, and therefore he gave my number to the lottery agent to call me directly. In no time I heard my phone belling with a strange number. I answered the call, and it was someone called Edem on the line, who claimed to be a lottery agent calling from Accra. "OK, how can I help you?"

"You won the American lottery," he replied.

"American lottery? How is that possible when I didn't enter it?"

"You remember your first year at UDS? You guys were in a queue for registration, and shortly after the registrations someone took your passport pictures and your particulars?"

"Oh yes!" I recalled.

"This is how it comes that today I am calling you."

"Oh OK." I made the arrangements to meet him.

The following week I left Gambibgo to go to Accra to join a brother to go together to meet Edem because I was afraid to go alone. We met Edem, and everything was confirmed to be true. Edem said that he would be charging $5,000 for the processing fee and his allowance. Where was I—someone who could not pay his school fees—going to get $5,000? I consulted people, and a lot of funds were raised from well-wishers and family members. The visa was secured, and I went back to school, changed my course and set everything up to go to America. At that moment it seemed to me like I was dreaming. Even while I was in the air, I kept touching myself to check that I was not asleep. But in God everything is always possible.

I arrived in New Jersey, where I waited for my green card and for my social security to arrive from the Department of Homeland Security. I was always on Facebook, and on the Ghana web, and listening to online Ghana radios just to try to keep up with what was going on in Ghana. One morning, I logged on to the Ghana web, and I read an article concerning one of the villages in the Volta Region (VR) of Ghana.

A Muslim child was sick, and he had been sent to the hospital on his arrival in the village. The child was without health insurance, and the doctors refused to treat him. His parents went away to try to raise money. By the time that they had come back, their child had given up his soul to the ghost. The Muslims started causing violence at the hospital, beating up the doctors and other hospital staff. The chief of the village became upset and said that the child would not be buried on his land. In Ghana, the land belongs to chiefs; each chief owns his community and all of its resources. While the body was in the morgue, another imam died, and as custom demands that Muslims are buried the same day that they die, the Muslim community quickly rushed the dead body to the cemetery and laid him to rest. Because of the anger that the Muslims caused at the hospital, the chief was still upset and decided to order people to dig out the dead body of the imam and put the body on the street.

This generated a tribal and ethnic war between the Muslim community/the zongo community and the indigenes of Hohoe in the VR. In the absence of the chief, the Muslims went and destroyed properties at the palace. When the chief returned from Accra, he was mad, and he asked Muslims in the village to move out since, he argued, they did not belong to the community.

In Ghana, all zongo communities are made up of Muslims who are believed to be immigrants from elsewhere. However, history tells us that they had lived in that village for three hundred years. Now my concern and my question is, does one become a first-class citizen of Ghana by birth or by virtue of the fact that the land that they occupy belongs to their forefathers? If that is the case, there would be no first-class Ghanaian, because history tells us that the members of every tribe in Ghana are immigrants.

*   *   *

As a peace-building and an educational book, I see it necessary to remind readers about similar occurrences in some parts of the world and their negative repercussions to their nations security

At this point I want to remind ourselves of the use of tribal comments that can plunge a nation into chaos and compare the status quo to our African neighbouring countries and even some parts of Europe during the 1930s where similar processes occurred and where they never tasted peace in their days of turmoil. Our individual cultures may suggest division by trying to look down upon others, but I believe that Ghana is a Christian country and that we still stick to our Christian values. God through his prophets in the good book created all under equal rights and opportunities. These issues of tribalism and racism are not only existent in children and illiterates who are believed to be lacking knowledge, but even in our politicians and leaders who are supposed to act responsibly and live by example. They can be the embodiment of divisions based on tribal, religious, and sectional grounds.

We live in a country where law-making bodies, the so-called politicians who are supposed to make laws to protect women and minorities, pass bills and develop budgets that can create jobs for the ever-increasing unemployed graduates who keep piling up every year, sit rather at the parliament house demanding huge pay and using words like "cocoa ase kuraseni", meaning a village cocoa boy, to describe themselves, instead of concentrating on the work for which they were elected.

The irresponsible nature of our leaders has also led some citizens who are misled by them to act lawlessly. For instance, a friend of mine told me a story in this regard about his grandfather. He said that during one electioneering year, his granddad had his land given out to some northerners who had migrated to the south in search of shelter. When it was election year in 2004, the northerners came out of the village to vote, but they were prevented from expressing their franchise by their landlord who happened to be an Ashanti. He told them to vote for the NPP, the supposed Ashanti party. The northerners agreed to do so, but the landlord suspected that they would still vote for the NDC in reality since they were from the north and thus told them not to vote at all and that failure to comply would lead to termination. He said that he would get his land back if he saw a drop of an ink on their thumbs. Because they were scared of losing their daily bread, they were denied their franchise, something that is a citizenship right.

The goal of citing these instances is not to produce a campaign manifesto but rather to let readers understand that politics will always suggest tribalism and racism. However, how we handle it and control our emotions in order to maintain peace is what should matter in every election.

There is no doubt that racism has been an issue in every campaign across the world, Ghana is also neither the first nor the last country to be tribalistic in its campaign. It happens everywhere in the globe. Even in America, a land of immigrants from different parts of the world, which is supposed to be an embodiment of democracy, racism exists in the elections.

If racism did not exist then Obama would not have received more than 90 per cent of the black vote. Equally, there were racist comments levelled against Obama. I listened to a YouTube video, and his rivals spoke of how he was not black enough to be president. Some said that he is brown. And that is not to mention the many profane words that were used to describe him. However, the difference is that you don't see extreme reactions to this. You do not see violence escalating out of these comments. America came together after its election for nation building and development, which is where I want our nation to be.

In our case, after every election there is an increase in the price of goods every single day in our markets across the whole nation. The price hikes are not always because of the new government's policies but frequently represent the attempts of those who are not on the government's side to sabotage the government.

THE RWANDAN GENOCIDE

This second part of the book talks about how tribal and racial discrimination crippled down some economies and twisted the lives of women and children specifically in Africa and some part of the world, because people vying for political positions in society would do everything at all cost to achieve their dreams, even if they have to incite people to fight for them, An example of a similar situation that nearly occurred in Ghana is the most recent incident when one law-maker was secretly caught on tape inciting some young people to wage a tribal war against the Voltarians and the Gas. Luckily enough, before the perpetrator could realize that his actions had become the object of public ridicule, he was brought before the court to face the consequences. That court case is currently pending. In view of that, I try to discuss in some detail here the causes and its effects on those economies and the lives of the people. I hope and believe that this will in a way deter people from involving themselves in such acts in the near future. I will start with one of our next-door neighbours:

Rwanda.

The months of April and June in 1994 saw a massacre that led to the deaths of approximately eight hundred thousand people in Rwanda within a period of one hundred days.

Most of them were Tutsis—with the perpetrators being Hutus. Let's find out ahead what led to this turmoil and draw lines of comparison to the status quo in Ghana to find out if there is a likelihood of it happening in Ghana.

Ethnic massacre in Rwanda is nothing new. There has always been misunderstanding between the majority Hutus and the minority Tutsis, but the hatred between the two has increased progressively since the colonial era.

Although they all speak the same language, inhabit the same areas, and follow the same traditions, in general the Tutsis are taller and thinner than the Hutus, with some speculating that they were originally from Ethiopia, and colonial masters gave greater recognition to Tutsis. The Belgians considered the Tutsis to be superior to the Hutus. Not surprisingly, the Tutsis welcomed this idea, and for the next twenty or so years they enjoyed better jobs and educational opportunities than their Hutu counterparts.

Resentment among the Hutus gradually built up, culminating in a series of riots in 1959. More than twenty thousand Tutsis were killed around this time, and many more fled to the neighbouring countries of Burundi, Tanzania, and Uganda.

When Belgium relinquished power and granted Rwanda independence in 1962, the Hutus took their place. Over subsequent decades, the Tutsis were portrayed as the scapegoats for every crisis.

Over time the Tutsis began to express that they did not believe that the Hutus deserved to handle the top public offices, and so elections were based on tribal lines. This reminds me of a conversation with my fellow Ghanaian, who happened to be an Ashanti, with respect to the violence that escalated after the election. The opposition, generally believed to be a party of the Ashanti tribe, lost the election with a popular majority vote of more than 320,000 representing 50.7 per cent, and yet that opposition would not concede and filed a suit against the incumbent and the electoral commission at the Supreme Court of Ghana for electoral malpractice. The same party lost in the 2008 election with a difference of just forty thousand votes and conceded immediately. Why not now?

One could be right if he or she associates the situation with tribalism. In 2008 the incumbent was an Akan, which is part of the Ashanti descent in the southern part of Ghana. In this year, however, the incumbent was from the opposite part of the country, the north. This tribe has been regarded by the Ashantis as illiterates, as farmers, as uncivilized, and as not worthy to be trusted with public office, but to their surprise, the incumbent won. They therefore believed that probably something had gone wrong somewhere, that there had been some rigging of the elections, and they talked of going to court for clarification. This analysis came as a result of comments that came up during the campaign season, with some members of the opposition making public declarations that they would not vote for the incumbent because of his tribe, with the common reason being that the northern tribe is noted for farming and herdsmanship.

During our discussion about the current situation in Ghana, Mr Marfo, my Ashanti friend, told me that the Ashanti tribe is regarded worldwide, even by our colonial masters, and that therefore they should constitute the executive arm of our government. He said that even the Queen of England could extend an invitation to the overlord of the Ashanti to Buckingham Palace for a get-together. He asked me how many chiefs from the north have ever been invited by the British queen. I couldn't name any because there is none. This is because in the olden days the Ashanti Empire was the most powerful empire in Ghana. They were rich in gold and all the mineral resources as well as cocoa and timber. The colonial masters first traded with the Ashantis. The only encounter I believe they had with the north was slave trade because they had the "giant people" by then. This colonial recognition and animosity between the tribes of Ghana started during colonialism. Like in Rwanda.

As Ghanaians, the Rwandan genocide should be a lesson for us to not repeat the mistakes that were made. In Rwanda, the consequence was massacre, with the bodies of Tutsis thrown into rivers and their killers saying that they were being sent back to Ethiopia. Young people's lives became twisted. With women and children seeking refuge in neighbouring countries, a lack of education resulted, affecting children and many more.

Even for a country with such a turbulent history as Rwanda, the scale and speed of the slaughter left its people reeling.

The genocide was sparked by the death of the Rwandan president Juvenal Habyarimana, a Hutu, when his plane was shot down above Kigali Airport on 6 April 1994.

A French judge blamed the Rwandan President Paul Kagame—at the time the leader of a Tutsi rebel group—and some of his close associates for carrying out the rocket attack.

Mr Kagame vehemently denies this, saying that it was the work of Hutu extremists, in order to provide a pretext to carry out their well-laid plans to exterminate the Tutsi community.

Whoever was responsible, within hours a campaign of violence spread from the capital throughout the country, a campaign that did not subside for three months.

But the death of the president was by no means the only cause of Africa's largest genocide in modern times. In the years before the genocide the economic situation was worsening and the incumbent president, Juvenal Habyarimana, was losing popularity.

At the same time, Tutsi refugees in Uganda—supported by some moderate Hutus—were forming the Rwandan Patriotic Front (RPF), led by Mr Kagame. Their aim was to overthrow Habyarimana and secure their right to return to their homeland.

Habyarimana chose to exploit this threat as a way to bring dissident Hutus back to his side, and Tutsis inside Rwanda were accused of being RPF collaborators.

In August 1993, after several attacks and months of negotiation, a peace accord was signed between Habyarimana and the RPF, but it did little to stop the continued unrest.

When Habyarimana's plane was shot down at the beginning of April 1994, it was the final nail in the coffin.

Exactly who killed the president—and with him the president of Burundi and many chief members of staff—has not been established.

Whoever was behind the killing, its effect was both instantaneous and catastrophic.

In the month of July, the RPF invaded Kigali. The regime collapsed, and the RPF declared a ceasefire because their goal had been achieved.

Soon after, it became clear that the RPF had been successful. Roughly two million Hutus fled to Zaire, which could possibly now be called the Democratic Republic of Congo (DR Congo).

These refugees were large in number and have since suffered from massacres.

In an attempt to provide a lasting solution, a multi-ethnic government was set up, with a Hutu, Pasteur Bizimungu, as president and Mr Kagame as his vice. Let us see if this could possibly solve the problem of tribal and racial discrimination.

The pair later broke out with Bizimungu being jailed on the grounds of inciting ethnic violence, while Mr Kagame became substantive.

Although the killing in Rwanda was said to be done, the presence of Hutu militias in DR Congo has caused so many years of turmoil there, causing up to five million deaths.

Rwanda's now Tutsi-led regime has on two occasions invaded its most dominant neighbour, saying that it wants to relegate the Hutu forces.

The Congolese Tutsi rebel group has remained active, refusing to give up its arms, arguing that it would place its community at risk of genocide.

Again several attempts have being put in place to remedy the situation, with the existence of numerous peace-keeping forces. However, they have been unable to end the fighting.

Source: BBC News (n.d.) 'Rwanda: How the genocide happened', *BBC Homepage*, 17 May 2011.

THE APARTHEID IN
SOUTH AFRICA

What about the apartheid system in South Africa? I will need to keep the commentary short.

As the continent of Africans moved to independence, the white population in South Africa still aimed at maintaining their way of life, which to them meant maintaining power. In other words, they still wanted to maintain the ideology of white superiority and black inferiority, and they wanted to continue to deny the black man power.

These whites, who are of British and Dutch descent, accounted for about 20 per cent of the population. There were also Asians, mainly Indians, who constituted 2 per cent. Blacks were the majority—about 70 per cent. Those grouped as the "Molato" (mixed race) made up 8 per cent. The conservative whites—many of whom were farmers of Dutch origin, considered it to be a God-given right to rule the blacks and saw no reason to give up ruling them.

Not only did the white farmers depend on the blacks' cheap labour for farming, but manufacturers also took advantage of the cheap labour of the blacks. The fast-growing South Africa was made up of 50 per cent of the black population living in cities dominated by white governments, most of them working as semi-skilled labour in manufacturing, operating machinery as a substitute for the white master-craftsmen of their predecessors. The labour of blacks had become the backbone of South Africa's economy, but with wage discrimination. A law was enacted giving rise to what they termed the Civilized Labour Policy, which protected the wage levels of white workers and left employers free to hire blacks at wages as low as possible. Another act, called the Bantu Act of 1953, took schools away from missions and assured that whites would receive an education that was different from and superior to that of blacks.

Movement of blacks in the urban areas exacerbated race relations, and in 1948 the most conservative of white political parties, the Nationalist Party, won the national election—an election that was not ran on fair grounds because only whites participated. The Nationalist Party predominately consisted of those from rural areas and of Dutch lineage, and it was the most popular in terms of maintaining a separation between whites and the other races in South Africa.

They even did what was more than maintaining the separation of the races. Although blacks were working in white-owned factories, in other white businesses, and in white homes, they abided by restrictions (that were common in the South in the United States), such as having their own points of entry into public places and, in the cities, they largely divided into black enclaves. However, there was yet too much integration for the Nationalist Party.

Legislation served to restrict blacks living in cities. They couldn't own their own homes for themselves in urban areas; they had to rent abandoned houses from local administration boards. The old apartheid doctrine that blacks were "temporary sojourners" or temporal residers in the cities was in use. In addition, while those who had worked for the same employer for ten years or for different employers for fifteen years were allowed to continue living in cities and towns all others were considered as "the undocumented" and had to have special work permits, which were subject to renewal on a yearly basis.

The so-called black ghettos in South Africa's cities were erased. This meant neighbourhoods of mixed races residing with one another. Blacks were required to move with identification cards, which were open to inspection by any police officer or agent of the government when the need arose. Blacks had to acquire visas for travel in order to undertake various activities.

In responding to the Nationalist Party's policies, the blacks increased agitation. An organization by the name of the African National Congress (ANC) turned to strikes and civil disobedience.

At this juncture I will try to draw some connections between this situation and that in Ghana. Something similar happens in Ghana today but indirectly. To acquire a good-paying job in Ghana today is determined by which section of Ghana one comes from. The "it's not what you know it's who you know" system is the order of the day. In effect some end up feeling that they are not being treated fairly: They do not have a relative in some top-most position and, thus they are finding it very hard to get a job. At some point in time, job-seekers have to identify themselves with a political party before being hired. Furthermore, purchasing land to build a house can sometimes be based on one's tribe. The situation is devastating. But how different is it from the apartheid? Ours is indirect, but it is gradually growing and will continue to do so if care is not taken.

In 1956, the South African regime indicted 156 opposition leaders, including the hero in African politics Nelson Rolihlahla Mandela, the then leader of the African National Congress. The African National Congress released what it called a Freedom Charter, stressing that South Africa belonged to all who lived in it—black, white, blue, or green—and calling for universal suffrage and individual freedoms and rights similar to those of the US Bill of Rights.

Guess what, the British government was less than convinced over the new repressions in South Africa, and a white majority approved a new constitution that in 1961 made South Africa a republic, having received so many sanctions from the world. South Africa's government had hoped to keep consolidating its relationship with the Commonwealth, but with criticism from other Commonwealth nations South Africa withdrew its membership.

I remember the story of the sanctions that the United Nations (UN) and other international organizations put on South Africa. Yet the then Ghanaian prime minister, Professor Kofi Abrefa Busia, kept the Ghanaian relationship with South Africa to the neglect of the decisions taken by the international organizations. This caused the military regime to overthrow the prime minister with the reason that the prime minister had disgraced the nation and disowned the international organizations by associating itself with the apartheid South Africa.

In the 1960s, South Africa had economic growth second only to that of Japan. Trade with Western countries grew, and investors from the United States, France, and Britain rushed in to try to get a piece of the action. Resistance among blacks had been crushed. Since 1964, Mandela, leader of the African Nation Congress, had been in prison on Robben Island just off the coast from Capetown, and it appeared that South Africa's security forces could handle any resistance to apartheid. However, in the 1970s this rosy picture for South Africa's whites began to fade.

In 1974, resistance to apartheid was encouraged by Portugal's withdrawal from Mozambique and Angola. Portugal could not afford to continue combating liberation movements in its colonies, which were being aided by the Soviet Union and China. South African troops withdrew from Angola in early 1976, failing to prevent the liberation forces from gaining power there, and black students in South Africa celebrated a victory of black liberation over white resistance.

That same year, South Africa's Nationalist Party passed a law prohibiting instruction in schools to be in any language but Africkaans and English. In the town of Soweto, a student demonstration protesting against this move was fired upon by the police, and a 13-year-old student was killed. People in Soweto were outraged, and for three days war existed between the outraged public and the police. The clashes then spread to other black townships. Two whites died and at least 150 blacks, mostly school children. The liberation movement among blacks spread to teachers, churchmen, and so forth.

In 1978 the defence minister of the Nationalist Party, Pieter Willem Botha, became prime minister. Botha's white regime was worried about the Soviet Union helping revolutionaries in South Africa, and the economy had turned sluggish. The new government noted that it was spending too much money trying to maintain the segregated homelands that had been created for blacks and that the homelands were proving to be uneconomic.

During that time, maintaining blacks as a third class became a thing of the past. The labour of blacks remained vital to the economy, and illegal black labour unions were flourishing. Many blacks remained too poor to make much of a contribution to the economy through their purchasing power—although they represented more than 70 per cent of the population. Capitalism functioned on goodwill, and it was goodwill with which Botha's regime was most concerned—not for the sake of capitalism so much as that it was afraid that an antidote was needed to prevent the blacks from being attracted to Communism.

Although Botha was strongly concerned about the popularity of Mandela, and denounced him as an arch-Marxist committed to violent revolution, to appease black opinion and to nurture ideas of Mandela as a respectable leader of black people, the government moved Mandela from the Robben Island to a more pleasant prison in a rural area just outside of Capetown: Pollsmoor Prison. That was a place open to visitors and well-wishers including interviews by foreigners—to let the world know that Mandela was being treated well.

To please the blacks and to regain its international relationship against apartheid, a new constitution was created. Black homelands were declared nation-states, and by-laws were abolished. Also, black labour unions were legitimized. The government recognized the rights of blacks to live in big cities and to act as owners and gave blacks property rights. Interest was expressed in rescinding the laws that existed against marriages between races (and sexes), which were under ridicule abroad. The government committed itself to "separate but equal" education, and the spending for black schools increased (to only one-seventh of what it was for white children per child, but up from one-sixteenth in 1968). At the same time, attention was given to strengthening the effectiveness of the police apparatus.

The anti-apartheid movements in the United States and in Europe were gaining support for boycotts against South Africa, for the withdrawal of US firms from South Africa, and for the release of

Mandela. South Africa was becoming an outlaw in the world community of nations. Investing in South Africa by Americans and others was coming to an end.

In January 1985, Botha addressed the government's House of Assembly and stated that the government was willing to release Mandela under certain conditions. Mandela's reply was read in public by one of his allies to embrace all conditions in as much as apartheid was over—his first words distributed publicly since his sentence to prison twenty-one years before. Mandela described violence as the responsibility of the apartheid regime and said that with democracy there would be no need for violence. Supporters cheered him, and he was ascended to being the leader of the black movement in South Africa and subsequently the first black president of South Africa.

Botha's effort to win hearts and minds failed. If anything, other than the white minority were encouraged to seek more than what was offered by Botha's reforms, doing otherwise, many believed, would make them function as tools for black power. The campaign to overthrow apartheid escalated, with African National Congress leaders in exile calling for consumer abolishment and the people's war to make townships ungovernable. Violence increased, and rage was mounted by police officers who were blacks and township officials regarded as state comedians. Other black-on-black violence escalated between the followers of the opportunistic Zulu chieftain and supporters of the ANC.

The Prime Minister blamed the violence in the townships on Communist demonstrators and the international media. A state of emergency was pronounced. The police were ordered to move against "troublemakers", and special attention shifted to student activism. People were rounded up and, out of sight of the public, prisoners were tortured. Some were killed slowly by rat poison being added to their food—events later documented. In 1989, four thousand deaths were reported, mostly blacks.

By 1987 the growth of South Africa's economy had dropped to among the lowest of the rates in the world, and the ban on South African participation in international sporting events was frustrating many whites in South Africa. Examples of African states with black leaders and white minorities existed in Kenya and Zimbabwe. Dreamers dreamt of South Africa having a black president, which became a reality. Mandela was moved to a four-bedroom house of his own, with a swimming pool and decorated by Abies trees, on a prison farm just outside of Capetown. He had an unpublicized meeting with Botha, Botha impressing Mandela by walking forward and exchanging Mandela's tea as a symbol of reconciliation. And the two had a friendly discussion, Mandela comparing the African National Conference's rebellion with that of the Afrikaaner rebellion, and talking about everyone being brothers. South Africa's economy would have been built more than it is today had it prevented the apartheid system, but it is still the best African economy.

THE HOLOCAUST

And finally, I would like to cite one example from Europe. Another great empire and kingdom fell as a result of racism or lack of value for one another with the holocaust between the Germans and the Jews. After its concession in World War I, Germany was humiliated by the Versailles Treaty, which reduced its pre-war jurisdiction, drastically reduced its military base, asked the country to recognize its guilt for the war, and stipulated that it pay reparations to the allied powers. With the German Empire destroyed, there was a formation of a new congressional government called the Weimar Republic. The republic experienced economic turbulence, which increased during the worldwide depression after the New York stock market crash in 1929. Massive inflation coupled with high unemployment heightened existing class and political differences and began to undermine the government.

Adolf Hitler, the then leader of the National Socialist German Workers (Nazi) Party, was pronounced chancellor of Germany by the president Paul Von Hindenburg on 30 January 1933. The Nazi Party had achieved a significant victory of the total vote cast in the elections of 1932.

The Nazis incited clashes with the Communists and conducted a vicious propaganda campaign against its political opponents—the weak Weimar Government and the Jews, whom the Nazis blamed for Germany's ills.

Among some of the propaganda levelled against the Jews was the weekly Nazi newspaper (*The Atmtacker*). At the bottom of the front page of each issue, in bold letters, the paper declared: "The Jews are our problems!" The attacker also used cartoons as representatives of Jews in which they were personified as hooked-nosed and apelike. The influence of the newspaper was far-reaching: By 1938 about half a million copies were made available to the public on a weekly base.

I would like to chip in here with a comparison in Ghana. Some Akans claim that whenever the opposite party NDC comes to power they leave our economy with debt because they believe that since that party mostly consists of northerners, they are thieves, armed robbers, and poor people, and therefore when they come to power they try to fill up their pockets before thinking of the nation.

Soon after Hitler became chancellor, he called for new elections in an attempt to gain full influence of the Reichstag, the German parliament, for the Nazis. The Nazis used the government equipment to attack the other parties. The Nazis put the other parties' leaders into political detention and forced the parties to cease from meetings. Then, in the midst of the election campaign, on 27 February 1933, the Reichstag building burned. A Dutchman by the name of Marinus van der Lubbe was arrested for the crime, and he insisted that he had acted alone. Although many suspected that the Nazis were mainly the perpetrators, the Nazis had a way of blaming the Communists, thus turning more votes to their favour.

The fire indicated the collapse of German democracy. On the next day, the government, under the intention of controlling the Communists, abrogated individual rights and protections: freedom of the press, assembly, and expression were abolished, as well as the right to privacy. When the elections were held on 5 March, the Nazis had about 44 per cent of the vote, and only 8 per cent went to the Conservatives. The Nazis therefore won a majority in the government.

The Nazis moved quickly to consolidate their power into an authoritative form of government. On 23 March they enacted an act that gave several sanctions to Hitler's authoritarian efforts and mandated him legally to pursue them further. The Nazis gathered their strong propaganda machinery to sideline their critics. They also developed a sophisticated security made up of police and military bases.

The SA (Storm Troopers), an underground organization, helped Hitler to end the German democratic credentials. There was also a security group called the Gestapo (also known as the Secret State Police) who were trained by professional police officers and had the authority to arrest anyone after 28 February. The SS(Protection Squad) served as Hitler's personal security guards, and they eventually controlled the concentration camps. The SD (the Security Service of the SS) functioned as the Nazis' intelligence professionals, unveiling enemies and keeping them under surveillance.

Because of the above security systems being put in place by Hitler's administration, opponents were being maltreated, beaten, and/or detained. The Germans built Dachau, just outside of Munich, to detain them, the first of its sort to be built for political detainees. Dachau's purpose changed periodically, and finally it became another brutal concentration camp for Jews.

By the end part of 1934, Hitler's regime had polarized the whole of Germany, giving him total control and putting his campaign against the Jews into full swing. Hitler and his Nazis claimed that the Jews corrupted pure German culture with their "foreign" and "mongrel" influence. They viewed the Jews as evil and cowardly, and viewed Germans as hard-working, courageous, and honest.

This is the same as our current situation in Ghana, where some sections of the country see others as criminals, as cattle-rearers, or as herdsmen and as not capable of manning the affairs of the nation. This is likely to generate huge tensions in the country in the near future, as the young ones today watch and imitate what their leaders are doing.

The Jews, the Nazis claimed, weakened Germany's economy and tradition, although they were represented in finance, commerce, the press, literature, theatre, and the arts. The entire government-supported propaganda machine created a racial anti-Semitism that was different from the long-standing anti-Semitic tradition of the Christian churches.

The superior race, it was claimed, was the "Aryans", the Germans. The word "Aryan" is derived from the study of linguistics, which started in the eighteenth century and at some point determined that the Indo-Germanic (also known as Aryan) languages were superior in their structures, variety, and vocabulary to the Semitic languages that had evolved in the Near East. Do we have similar attitudes in Ghana? I am not going to mention names, as the purpose of this book was not to favour one particular section of the populace, but it was meant for peace building across all the ethnic groups in Ghana.

Source: Yahil, Leni (1990) *The Holocaust: The fate of European Jewry*, New York: Oxford University Press, p. 36.

Darfur Genocides

Similar to that of Ghana, Darfur is itself a very diverse place, made up of over 90 tribes and countless sub-clans. It is situated in western Sudan and covers an area the size of Texas, with a pre-conflict population of 6 million people. Darfur was an independent sultanate until it was added to Sudan by British forces in 1916 during the petition of Africa; however, it never received nearly the level of investment and development that Eastern Sudan and the Nile River Valley did under British rule. This marginalization continued under the string of central Sudanese governments that followed independence in 1956.

While the conflict in Darfur is most frequently described as one between genious "Arab" and "non-Arab" (or "African") tribes, the more accurate distinction between population groups in Darfur is not ethnic, but economic. The incredibly arid northern part of Darfur, populated mainly by tribes claiming "Arab" descent, developed an economy based on nomadic cattle—and camel-herding. The more arable south, where the majority of the population traces "non-Arab" i.e., "African" descent, developed a subsistence farming economy. Centuries of intermarriage and slave trading have blurred the lines between distinguishing physical ethnic characteristics, but for the most part this economic division remained unchanged.

Starting in the 1980s, drought, hunger and the spread of the deserts caused increased competition for land, severely upsetting the structure of Darfur society. Farmers had claimed every available bit of land to farm or forage for food, closing off traditional routes used by the herders. The herders, desperate to feed and water their animals in a dwindling landscape, tried to force the southern routes open, attacking farmers who tried to block their paths. Traditionally, conflicts were settled with little or no violence by respected local councils. These were abrogated by the Bashir regime after it came to power in a coup in 1989, leaving no mechanisms for resolving disputes peacefully.

Spurred by this increasing conflict over scarce resources and wedge politics played by the central government in Northern Sudan, nomadic and farming tribes began to polarize along ethnic lines. To Darfuris facing starvation, the dichotomous ideology of African versus Arab began to have explanatory power. Amongst some sedentary "Africans", the ideas that uncaring "Arabs" in Khartoum had let the famine happen and then Darfuri "Arabs" armed by their Libyan allies had attacked "African" farmers began to gain credence. Similarly, semi-nomadic Darfuri "Arabs" began to seriously consider that "Africans" had seriously tried to punish them for the famine by trying to keep them from pastureland.

For a number of years Darfur was the scene of sporadic clashes between "African" farming communities such as the Fur, Masalit and Zaghawa, on the one hand, and "Arab" nomadic groups on the other. These clashes lead to many deaths and to the destruction and looting of homes. The government blamed competition over scarce resources for the clashes, and in fact, did nothing to try to resolve the problems in Darfur.

In 2002-2004, Leadership of Darfuri were excluded from the US backed peace talks, considered unimportant in the context of the Second Sudanese Civil War. The proposed settlement agreement would ostensibly bring great economic development into Sudan, but none of the opportunity would benefit the people of Darfur. Darfuri leaders demanded political reform and economic assistance, but to no avail.

The conflict in Sudan's western Darfur region increased in 2003 when two rebel groups rose up against the government, accusing it of neglect. The government of Sudan moved swiftly to crush the revolt by the Justice and Equality Movement (JEM) and the Sudan Liberation Army (SLA).

The government's counterinsurgency campaign aimed to "get at the fish by draining the sea." Civilians of the same ethnic group as the rebels were the target for destruction, considered potential threats by the government for their potential kinship to and support of rebel armies. The government of Sudan armed militias, known as the Janjaweed ("evil man on horseback" in Arabic). The Janjaweed, drawn from Arab tribes, have used scorched-earth tactics against civilians similar to those used in the North/South Civil War. The Janjaweed are blamed for killings, widespread rape and abductions. Refugees describe them as ferocious gun-wielding men riding camels or horses who burn villages and steal whatever they can carry.

September 9, 2004, the US Secretary of State Colin L. Powell told the Senate Foreign Relations Committee, "genocide has been committed in Darfur and that the Government of Sudan and the Janjaweed bear responsibility—and that genocide may still be occurring." President George W. Bush echoed this in July 2005 when he stated that the situation in Darfur was "clearly genocide."

Analysts estimate that up to four hundred thousand civilians have been killed through war-related violence, disease and starvation. Women and girls are under particular threat as rape is used as a weapon of war and a tool of genocide. 2.7 million Civilians are internally displaced and an additional two hundred and fifty thousand live as refugees in neighboring countries such as Chad and the Central African Republic. Overall, 4.7 million conflict-affected people live in need of humanitarian relief for their daily survival.

Beginning 2008, a combined United Nations-African Union force took over peacekeeping in Darfur from a purely African Union force. The seven thousand-strong AU force had been massively overused and still unable to quell the violence or protect civilians. The U.N. Security Council authorized up to twenty six thousand troops and police for the new hybrid force, but as of March 2009, only sixty percent were on the ground. The resultant UNAMID (United Nations—African Union Mission in Darfur) force has been unable to fully protect civilians on the ground; despite a relatively strong peace-enforcement mandate, UNAMID is stymied at once by obstructionism on the part of the Sudanese government and lack of supplies, sourcing of funds for purchase of equipment by the international community.

Darfur Genocide. (n.d.). Retrieved from http://www. jewishworldwatch.org/conflictareas/sudan/overview/sudan-genocide

UNREALIZED DREAMS OF OUR FOUNDERS

An issue of mediocrity and failed policies in African governments and the way forward, to the rising stars

The political wave and wind that blew the Ghanaian saviour Dr Osagyefo Kwame Nkrumah to the soil of Ghana gave Ghana and Africa a great foundation that in my opinion could not be built up after his demise. Africa, a continent of fifty-two countries and that possesses the world's most important mineral resources, is still not independent today economically, although all of the countries in Africa today have gained political independence from the hands of colonial masters.

Our policies today are being dictated by the West and by international organizations like the UN, the World Bank, the World Health Organization (WHO), and the International Monetary Foundation (IMF) because when they provide us with all the aids and the loans for the development of Africa, they back it with their own conditions and policies that they believe to be good for us. We bear our own problems, and we are supposed to be the ones who know best our own problems, but we turn to leave them behind and execute policies in the interests of donors. Where is the economic independence?

Although politically we are allowed to choose political leaders on our own, which is the independence that our founders fought for, independence in my own opinion is still not complete when we cannot make and execute policies on our own devoid of foreign influence. This is a problem that I attribute to corrupt and weak leadership in the continent of Africa. The good foundation that was laid by our founders could not be sustained. Even the unity that was laid for us has been replaced with partisanship and improper coordination of African governments. In this book, I examine some of Nkrumah's effort to make Africa a union government with respect to a current "divided Africa" and the efforts of various governments to further divide our union.

Once upon a time, a visionary, charismatic, and radical son of Africa foresaw what would happen today in Somalia, Libya, Egypt, Sudan, Rwanda, and so forth and tried bringing us together but found that he was vehemently opposed by unpatriotic, non-nationalistic citizens. Although he was not successful in this fight, he did not end it there. Having worked tirelessly for the attainment of independence in almost thirty African countries during his tenure in office, he held several meetings and delivered numerous speeches in an attempt to make our continent a union nation.

As a unifier, he was dissatisfied with the results of all of the efforts he made for an independent Ghana. On the eve of our independence day, he said, "The independence of Ghana is meaningless unless there is the total liberation of the African continent," and today, I paraphrased his declaration to be "the democratic credentials of Ghana are incomplete and worthless unless there is the total attainment of democracy in all African nations". Nkrumah backed his words by deeds, and he made efforts to lead several African countries to emancipation. By the end of 1966, when he was overthrown, about thirty other African countries had achieved independence.

Today, Ghana, as we all know, is considered—in Ghana, Africa, and in parts of the international community—as the beacon of African democracy. I believe that we have got to do more in helping other countries to democratic governance than living by example though. We cannot say that we are democratic when our nextdoor neighbours have to lose lives before they transition to a new government. I am referring to the situation in the Ivory Coast, where, when it was a collective decision by African governments to contribute troops to overthrow by force the then illegitimate government, Ghana refused to contribute and told the African Union (AU) and the rest of the international community "Dziwo fie asem", which literally means, "Cry your own cry".

To me, it's about time that Africa came together to solve its own problems instead of depending on the West for development. As a student of development, I see development to be inside-out and not outside-in.

The West, which we consider to be the Jack-of-all-trades, can sometimes be the master of none when it comes to Africa's affairs. These are two continents with different cultures and different mentalities; we must be the drivers of our own development.

All of what I have described above makes me believe in Dr Nkrumah's statement that "the lack of a solution to Africa's problems of poverty, war, and over-exploitation of its resources are due to colonialism and lack of unity in the African continent". I believe that the only way for Africa to gain economic emancipation just as we have achieved political emancipation would be by the countries of Africa forming a more perfect union. That is the only way that we can own ourselves in all of our endeavours and even champion the whole world.

To me it is sometimes embarrassing to see African Union leadership sit down for the West to intervene in our affairs before there can be stability and peace on our land. I am referencing in particular the case of the Ivory Coast, where France and the European Union (EU) had to intervene before there was a smooth transition, but not only that, we saw what went on in Libya, in Egypt, and in Sudan. Must we always be supported by the West before our problems can be solved? Until when will the West be there for us?

Personally, I don't think that a form of partial independence was what our founders had in mind when they laid down their lives in the fight for our emancipation.

In view of all of these concerns I intend to come out with a book entitled *Unrealised Dreams of our Founders: An Issue of Mediocrity and Failed Policies in African Governments and the way forward to the rising stars.*

This book discusses in detail some of the policies started by Dr Kwame Nkrumah, which if continued would have put Africa in a better position in the world today. It also provides specific references from Ghana since independence and discusses the status quo.

Printed in the United States
By Bookmasters